HARPY EAGLE VS. OCELOT

BY NATHAN SOMMER

BELLWETHER MEDIA • MINNEAPOLIS, MN

™

Torque brims with excitement
perfect for thrill-seekers of all kinds.
Discover daring survival skills, explore
uncharted worlds, and marvel at mighty
engines and extreme sports. In *Torque* books,
anything can happen. Are you ready?

This edition first published in 2024 by Bellwether Media, Inc.

No part of this publication may be reproduced in whole or in part without written
permission of the publisher. For information regarding permission, write to
Bellwether Media, Inc., Attention: Permissions Department,
6012 Blue Circle Drive, Minnetonka, MN 55343.

Library of Congress Cataloging-in-Publication Data

LC record for Harpy Eagle vs. Ocelot available at:
https://lccn.loc.gov/2023000639

Editor: Kieran Downs   Designer: Josh Brink

Printed in the United States of America, North Mankato, MN.

TABLE OF CONTENTS

THE COMPETITORS

The thick **rain forests** of South America are home to thousands of animals. Harpy eagles are **apex predators**. Even large **mammals** are often **prey** to these powerful birds.

Ocelots are also skilled **predators**. These cats move easily on land, in water, and in trees. Which predator is the toughest?

Harpy eagles are some of the largest **raptors** in the world. They have thick legs, long **talons**, and large **crests**. They weigh up to 20 pounds (9.1 kilograms). Their wingspans stretch up to 6.5 feet (2 meters) wide.

These birds are found in parts of Central America and South America. The eagles build nests more than 100 feet (30.5 meters) above the ground.

LARGER FEMALES

Female harpy eagles can weigh twice as much as males.

HARPY EAGLE PROFILE

```
0      2 FEET    4 FEET    6 FEET    8 FEET
```

WEIGHT
UP TO 20 POUNDS
(9.1 KILOGRAMS)

WINGSPAN
UP TO 6.5 FEET
(2 METERS)

HABITAT

RAIN FORESTS

HARPY EAGLE RANGE

■ RANGE

OCELOT PROFILE

LENGTH
**UP TO 35 INCHES
(88.9 CENTIMETERS)**

WEIGHT
**UP TO 35 POUNDS
(15.9 KILOGRAMS)**

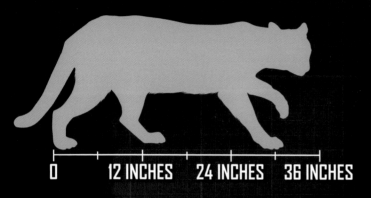

```
0        12 INCHES     24 INCHES     36 INCHES
```

HABITAT

RAIN FORESTS

GRASSLANDS

OCELOT RANGE

■ **RANGE**

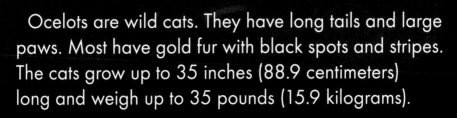

Ocelots are wild cats. They have long tails and large paws. Most have gold fur with black spots and stripes. The cats grow up to 35 inches (88.9 centimeters) long and weigh up to 35 pounds (15.9 kilograms).

Ocelots are found in parts of North America, Central America, and South America. These **nocturnal** cats live in rain forests and grasslands.

OCELOT COATS

No two ocelot coats are the same. Each one has a different pattern of spots!

9

SECRET WEAPONS

Harpy eagles have great eyesight. They can spot prey smaller than 1 inch (2.5 centimeters) long from more than 600 feet (182.9 meters) away! The birds easily find their meals.

Ocelots are built to hunt at night. Their eyes have a special layer that **reflects** light. This helps them see well in darkness.

Harpy eagles have broad wings. They help the eagles fly at speeds of up to 50 miles (80.5 kilometers) per hour! Most prey cannot escape them.

38 MILES (61.1 KILOMETERS) PER HOUR

OCELOT

28 MILES (45 KILOMETERS) PER HOUR

HUMAN

Ocelots use their strong legs to jump high. They pounce on prey. Their legs also help the cats run at speeds of up to 38 miles (61.1 kilometers) per hour.

SECRET WEAPONS

GREAT EYESIGHT

BROAD WINGS

LONG TALONS

HARPY EAGLE TALON

**5 INCHES
(12.7 CENTIMETERS)**

Harpy eagle talons grow up to 5 inches (12.7 centimeters) long. The birds use these to capture and kill prey. The talons are

OCELOT

REFLECTIVE EYES

STRONG LEGS

SHARP FANGS

FANG

Ocelots have sharp, pointed **fangs**. They use these to finish off prey. Special back teeth help the cats tear into meat.

ATTACK MOVES

Harpy eagles **ambush** their prey.
The eagles wait on their **perches** for the
perfect moment. Then they quickly dive!
The birds use their strong talons to grab prey.

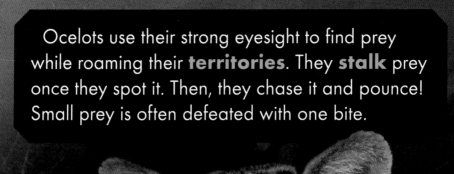

Ocelots use their strong eyesight to find prey while roaming their **territories**. They **stalk** prey once they spot it. Then, they chase it and pounce! Small prey is often defeated with one bite.

WATER HUNTERS

Ocelots do not just hunt on land. They can also catch fish right out of the water!

FLEXIBLE HEADS

Harpy eagles can turn their heads upside down. This helps them watch prey from every angle!

Harpy eagles squeeze small prey to break their bones. They fly away with it to eat in their nests. The eagles fly quickly up and down to hunt other birds in midair!

Ocelots arch their backs and lower
their tails straight down when threatened.
They claw and bite enemies in fights.
The cats climb trees to escape from danger.

READY, FIGHT!

A harpy eagle spots an ocelot from its perch. It dives in for a sneak attack. The ocelot claws the eagle. This allows the cat to climb a nearby tree.

But the eagle attacks again. It snatches the ocelot right off a tree branch! The ocelot was no match for the harpy eagle's powerful talons.

GLOSSARY

ambush—to carry out a surprise attack

apex predators—animals at the top of the food chain that are not preyed upon by other animals

crests—groups of feathers on the top of some birds' heads

fangs—long, pointed teeth

mammals—warm-blooded animals that have backbones and feed their young milk

nocturnal—active at night

perches—places where birds sit and rest

predators—animals that hunt other animals for food

prey—animals that are hunted by other animals for food

rain forests—thick, green forests that receive a lot of rain

raptors—large birds that hunt other animals; raptors are also called birds of prey.

reflects—gives back light

stalk—to follow closely and quietly

talons—sharp claws on birds that allow them to grab and tear into prey

TO LEARN MORE

AT THE LIBRARY

Hansen, Grace. *Ocelot*. Minneapolis, Minn.: Abdo Kids, 2023.

Lukidis, Lydia. *Eagles*. Mankato, Minn.: Black Rabbit Books, 2023.

Sommer, Nathan. *Golden Eagle vs. Great Horned Owl*. Minneapolis, Minn.: Bellwether Media, 2021.

ON THE WEB

FACTSURFER

Factsurfer.com gives you a safe, fun way to find more information.

1. Go to www.factsurfer.com

2. Enter "harpy eagle vs. ocelot" into the search box and click 🔍.

3. Select your book cover to see a list of related content.

INDEX

The images in this book are reproduced through the courtesy of: Andres Morya Hinojosa/ Alamy, front cover (harpy eagle); Joel Sartore/ Photo Ark/ Nature Picture Library, front cover (ocelot); Sohns/ Alamy, pp. 2, 20, 22 (ocelot); imageBROKER/ Hermann Breh, pp. 2-3, 20-21, 22-23 (harpy eagle); Dmitrii Kash, p. 4; slowmotiongli, p. 5; Mary Ann McDonald/ Getty, pp. 6-7, 12; Octavio Campos Salles/ Alamy, pp. 8-9; worldswildlifewonders, pp. 10, 18; Vladimir Cech, p. 11; Suzan Meldonian, p. 13; Beker Yepez, p. 14 (great eyesight); GTW, p. 14 (broad wings); Alfredo Maiquez, p. 14 (long talons); Chepe Nicolo, p. 14; Leonardo Mercon, p. 15 (reflective eyes); Saad315, p. 15 (strong legs); klublu, p. 15 (sharp fangs); Alejo Miranda, p. 15; Nick Garbutt/ Alamy, p. 16; Joe McDonald/ Getty, p. 17; Danita Delimont, p. 19.